Facing the Flood

Written by Sydnie Meltzer Kleinhenz
Illustrated by Winson Trang

STECK-VAUGHN
ELEMENTARY · SECONDARY · ADULT · LIBRARY

A Harcourt Classroom Education Company

www.steck-vaughn.com

Contents

The All-Star

Jesse Reyna rolled the smooth stone in his hand. He cocked his throwing arm behind his ear, dropped to his knees, and heaved the stone across the creek behind his house. Bam! The stone blasted bits of bark off the slender tree on the far bank.

He raised both arms in the air. "Out at second! Did you see that, Scooter? Another perfect throw for the all-star catcher!"

Scooter barked and jumped up, resting her muddy front paws against Jesse.

"Hey! No paws on the belt buckle!" Jesse scolded, pushing Scooter down gently. He used his shirt to wipe the mud from the buckle.

Jesse didn't hear his teenage sister, Sara, coming across the yard, until she spoke. "You love that belt buckle more than your dog," she teased.

"Scooter knows better," Jesse said, rubbing the dog's belly. "But I don't want any mud messing up my buckle." He pointed to the engraving. "Jesse Reyna, All-Star Catcher," he read aloud. "Not everybody gets to be on the all-star team. I had to work hard to get this buckle."

Sara nodded her head. "I know. I helped you practice. Listen. Gran's sink is stopped up, and Dad went to fix it. Mom went to get groceries before the rain comes. She said for you and me to stay put."

"Okay," Jesse replied. He pointed to the rising water in the creek. "Look how high the water's getting. It's almost up to the banks."

"It's all that rain they've had upstream," Sara said. "I hope it doesn't overflow." She ran toward the house. "Wipe your feet when you come in!"

Jesse was about to throw another stone across the creek when a gust of wind sent an empty trash can rolling across the yard. Scooter streaked after it like a hound after a rabbit. She caught up with the trash can, barking at it and blocking it with her shoulder. Jesse jogged over. "Good catch, girl."

Scooter wagged her little tail. Jesse squatted down to pet her. He was scratching behind her ears when he felt drops of rain tap his arm. He looked up at the sky and saw black storm clouds moving in. Another burst of wind swept the trash can into the whooshing creek. Scooter turned to chase after the can, but Jesse stopped her. Together they watched it float away.

A crack of thunder brought more rain. The sprinkle was quickly becoming a shower. Jesse dashed for the house with Scooter at his heels.

The Downpour

In the living room, Jesse watched his favorite Saturday morning TV show. Then he got out his baseball cards and sorted them as the rain grew heavier. Johnny Bench, Pudge Rodriguez, and Charles Johnson were his favorites. All of them were all-star catchers.

I'm an all-star, too, Jesse said to himself. He gazed down at his belt buckle and wondered if he'd see a Jesse Reyna baseball card someday.

Sara came in. "Jesse?"

"Hmm?" he answered.

"It's raining really hard now, and Mom's been gone for two hours. She should be home by now," Sara said with an uneasy look on her face.

Jesse looked outside. The street had deep puddles. The clock showed 10:20 in the morning, but the sky was growing darker and darker.

"Maybe it's taking her a long time to drive home in the rain," he said.

"I'm getting worried," Sara told Jesse. "Come look at the back yard."

"Why?" Jesse asked as he ran to the kitchen. He pressed his face against the window. "Oh, no," he said quietly. The creek was flooding over its banks, and rushing water was up to the swing set. More rain kept spilling from the sky.

"If the water is getting this high here, maybe it's covering the roads, too. Maybe Mom can't drive through it," Sara said. "I think I'd better call Dad."

As Sara punched in Gran's number, Jesse heard "Beep, beep, beep" from the TV. He ran into the living room and saw an emergency message on the screen. He read it aloud. "Flash flood warning until 6:00 P.M. High water will affect flood-prone areas. People are advised to take steps to protect lives and property."

"This is bad," Jesse said to Sara. Sara gripped the back of a chair.

"We just went from bad to worse," she added. "Our phone line is dead."

Jesse let out his breath in a big sigh. "Uh-oh."

Sara turned the TV volume up and flipped through the channels until she found a special report.

"Look at that," Jesse told Sara when he saw a diagram of the storm system on TV. "The storm has stalled over us. We've gotten nine inches of rain in three hours!"

Sara flipped to the next channel just in time to hear a weather reporter. "People in low areas and those near creeks and rivers should seek higher ground," said the woman in a serious voice.

Sara and Jesse looked at each other. Then they dashed to the kitchen window. The creek water was inching toward the back door.

"What are we going to do?" asked Jesse.

Sara bit her lip. "We have to go upstairs. Get some food and water and candles and anything special you want to save. I'm getting my new CD player."

Jesse put his hand on his all-star buckle. His most valuable possession was in a safe place. It would never get lost in a flood. He watched the new lawn chairs on the patio begin to rock in the water. *I'd better bring those chairs in so they don't get washed away,* he said to himself. Then he opened the back door.

The wild creek water was rushing across most of the patio. Jesse grabbed the two lawn chairs, but a cushion toppled into the flow. Scooter raced out the door to go after it.

"Scooter, no! Don't go near that water!" Jesse shouted, but it was too late. The little dog ran, then swam to fetch the cushion. Her teeth had just closed on it and Jesse had almost reached her. Then a gush of creek water swept her several feet away. Scooter let go of the cushion and gave a frightened little whine. Jesse screamed for Sara and got ready to charge into the flood water to save Scooter.

The Ride

Sara heard Jesse's shout and dashed down to the back door. She saw Jesse half-running and half-swimming across the yard toward Scooter. "Jesse, come back!" she yelled.

"It's okay! I've almost got her!" Jesse shouted back. He lunged forward, caught Scooter's leg, and pulled the dog toward him.

Sara plopped her CD player on the kitchen table and cried out, "Grab the swing set and hold on to it! I'll come and get you!" Moving quickly, she pushed herself into the fast-flowing water. Jesse grabbed Scooter with one hand and wrapped his legs around the swing set.

Sara was halfway to Jesse when a powerful surge of water knocked her off her feet. She fell into the water and paddled toward Jesse with all her might.

"Here, grab my hand!" yelled Jesse.

Sara gripped Jesse's outstretched hand, but a mighty current now swirled around the swing set, and it overtook them. It swept Sara, Jesse, and Scooter out of the yard and into the deep water of the flooded creek.

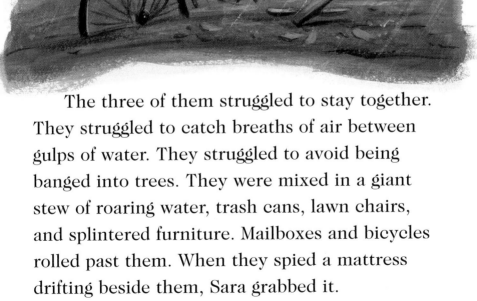

The three of them struggled to stay together. They struggled to catch breaths of air between gulps of water. They struggled to avoid being banged into trees. They were mixed in a giant stew of roaring water, trash cans, lawn chairs, and splintered furniture. Mailboxes and bicycles rolled past them. When they spied a mattress drifting beside them, Sara grabbed it.

Jesse tucked Scooter under one arm and piled on. Then Sara jumped on. Together the three rode the mattress down the creek that had become a roaring river.

At first they felt safe on the mattress. Jesse used his belt to make a kind of leash to keep Scooter safe. But then they entered a wide, flat area with no trees or buildings to block the strong storm wind. It whipped the flood water into a wild dance. The water tipped the mattress up, and Jesse lost his grip on the belt. In an instant, Scooter slid off the mattress and into the creek.

"Scooter! Come back, girl!" Jesse yelled. He and Sara tried to grab Scooter, but the creek was moving too fast. The current swept the little dog into the branches of a small uprooted tree.

"We've got to scoot back or we'll fall in, too!" Sara yelled. The mattress bounced and spun around and lodged in the low branches of a large, sturdy oak.

Jesse and Sara saw that Scooter was floating away from them. "Jesse, don't call her," Sara warned. "She's safer floating in those branches than she is trying to swim back." She spoke quickly. "Maybe she'll find her way home when the flood goes down. I've heard of dogs who got lost on vacation and still found their way home."

Jesse heard the doubt behind Sara's words. "Yeah," he said. "She's pretty smart, and she knows how to swim." They watched as Scooter disappeared around the bend.

Sara looked at Jesse with sad eyes. "I'm sorry, Jesse," she said. "I'm sorry you lost your belt buckle, too."

Jesse's shoulders sagged. His eyes filled with tears. Neither one spoke for a while.

The mattress twisted and jiggled against the tree. The creek slapped them with cold water, soggy trash, and aluminum cans. They looked around in the rain. Along the banks of the creek, toppled trees and houses lay half-covered by the dirty water. The houses bore scars where shutters and gutters had been torn off.

"The mattress is sinking," Jesse said. "We have to move." He scooted up closer to the branches. "Grab the tree," Jesse urged Sara. She reached for a branch.

The branch moved in her hand. Sara yelled and jumped away. Jesse saw her face go white.

"Aghhhh! Snake!" she screamed.

A large snake dropped on the mattress and began crawling toward his sister.

17

Without thinking, Jesse grabbed the snake by the tail and hurled it away as fast as Benito Santiago picking off a runner. Then he realized what he had touched and started shaking.

Sara huddled in a far corner of the mattress. She glanced at the upper branches and went even whiter. "Jesse, look up! The tree is full of snakes!"

Jesse scooted away from the tree.

"It looks like we went from bad to worse to horrible," he said.

"I'm scared," said Sara. "The creek snatched Scooter. We aren't safe by this tree, and this mattress won't hold us much longer."

Jesse swallowed hard. "I hope Scooter is safe somewhere," he replied. He wiped his eyes.

A piece of the mattress washed away. They sank deeper into the water.

"Sara, what are we going to do?" asked Jesse.

"The game's not over till the last out," she answered, trying to sound convincing. "We can think of something."

Jesse looked around. The wind had died down a little, and the downpour was slowing to a drizzle. But the creek sped along like a subway gone out of control.

"I think the rain is letting up. If it quits, the creek will start to go down," Jesse said. "Ouch!" He slapped at his foot. "Something's stinging me!"

Sara looked down. "Fire ants!" she yelled. She hurriedly started brushing the poison ants off Jesse's ankles and legs. "I can't believe these nasty things survive in a flood! There's a whole swarm of them in the water!"

"They're probably like us. They're trying to get to dry land," Jesse observed. He tried to splash the floating ant swarm away from the tree trunk, but the swirls in the current brought them back to the mattress.

"Ow!" said Sara, brushing herself off.

Jesse scanned the churning water. "Snakes are in the tree. Fire ants are attacking us. The mattress is falling apar—" He couldn't believe his eyes. In the water rushing toward them lay a large wooden gate. It looked strong enough to hold both of them. "See that gate?" he shouted to Sara. "Jump for it!"

They landed close enough to the gate to grab it. Quickly they pulled themselves onto it. The gate wobbled, and rough wood scraped their arms. But once Jesse and Sara found a place in the center, the gate traveled like a sturdy raft.

"Whew!" Sara puffed. "I'm soaked again, but this gate is better than the mattress."

"Yeah," said Jesse, rubbing an aching arm. "No snakes, no ants. Now if we could just steer it to the bank."

Sara gripped Jesse's arm. "We're going to have to do something quick," she announced in a tight voice. "There's a bridge coming up!"

Jesse stared at the bridge dead ahead. The swollen creek was filling the area under it. "There's still a little space to go under it," he told Sara.

"If we lie down, could we make it?" she asked hopefully.

"I can't tell," Jesse answered. He leaned slightly over the edge of the gate to get a better look. The gate wobbled dangerously. One arm and leg fell in the water.

Sara grabbed him. "Come back to the middle. Stop making us zigzag."

"I didn't make us zigzag—" Jesse began to argue. Then he stopped. "Hey, do you think we could zigzag on purpose and get to the bank?"

"You mean steer ourselves in the right direction?" Sara asked.

"Right!" Jesse answered in an excited voice. "I'll push against the water on one side with my arm and leg."

"Like steering a canoe with a paddle!" Sara piped in.

Dry Land!

"Hang onto me," Jesse directed. He got on his stomach and tried to hold his left arm and leg straight out into the water. The current slapped him, banged him, and scraped him against the wood.

Sara pulled Jesse back to the center of the gate. "Don't try that again," she advised. "You're bleeding."

Jesse rubbed his sore leg. He stared at the debris piling up against the side of the bridge. "What if I grab a branch and steer with it?"

"I think the current will smack it out of your hands like it smacked your arm and leg," Sara answered.

"Have you got any other ideas?" Jesse questioned.

"Well," she said slowly, "maybe we could make the gate go in the right direction by putting all our weight on one side."

Jesse watched a chair smash into the pile of debris near the shore. "Let's try it," he urged. "Hurry!"

He and Sara scooted to one side. Their weight pushed that side of the gate underwater. Water pouring over the gate nearly forced them off. They scrambled back toward the center. The bridge was very close.

"Let's try rocking. Maybe we can change our course," said Sara. "Ready? Right, forward. Right, forward."

The wooden gate flopped and wobbled, still heading straight toward the bridge. Then it whirled wildly and rammed into the pile of debris. The front end jammed against a chair. The back end began to spin again.

"Let's get off this thing!" Sara shouted as she scrambled across the pile of broken branches, furniture, twisted metal, and other flood wreckage.

Jesse felt the gate spin loose under him. He leaped for a tree limb on the pile of debris. It shifted with his weight, and his legs dropped into the water. The gate scraped the bridge as it was pulled under. Jesse felt the current dragging him toward the bridge.

From the creek bank, Sara yelled, "Hang on!" She spotted an old, heavy rope in the debris and frantically snatched it up. She tossed one end to Jesse. He grabbed it and held on for dear life.

Slowly Sara pulled Jesse closer to her. Branches scratched and poked him, but he held on. He was dragged over old tires, boards, and leaking garbage bags that rocked and shifted under him. Shoes and clothing swirled about in a tangled mess.

Jesse stared at a belt tangled in the debris. The buckle end was hidden under a crumpled mailbox. Seeing the belt made him think of Scooter and his last sight of her as she was swept away from him by the flood waters. He swallowed hard. *I'm going to be safe, but what about Scooter?* he wondered.

27

"Come on, Jesse. You're almost there. You can do it!" Sara encouraged him. Steadily she pulled him up the pile of debris until she could reach down and grab his hands.

"We made it!" she cried. "We're on land!"

Jesse looked both ways down the road. "Scooter!" he called. "Here, girl! Come on, Scooter!"

But there was no answering bark.

Sara hugged Jesse tightly. "Scooter's a very smart dog," she said. "We got out of the creek, and I bet she did, too. I'll bet she stuffed herself on hamburgers and french fries at the Burgerland trash bin and went home to wait for us."

Jesse gave his sister a weak smile. "She does love french fries. Maybe you're right." But he didn't believe Scooter would be waiting for them, and he didn't think Sara did either.

"Hey, look!" cried Sara. "There's the shopping center. My school is around the corner. That means we're only about five miles away from home."

"Let's go home," Jesse said.

"It's a long walk," Sara said. "I'm exhausted, and you've got some bloody scrapes from that gate. Let's see if we can find a phone that works at the shopping center. Mom and Dad may be back home and worried about us."

"Okay," Jesse agreed. They turned toward the shopping center.

Under the bridge the monstrous creek roared on without them.

Shelter

Jesse and Sara trudged slowly through the knee-high water in the shopping center parking lot. Every store was closed, and there was no pay phone. They returned to the street. The drizzle faded to a sprinkle and then stopped as they turned the corner.

Jesse pointed. "Look! Something is going on at your school."

"I think they've set up an emergency shelter here," said Sara. The two of them walked faster.

"I'm so wet. I hope they have towels," said Jesse.

"And blankets. I'm so cold," said Sara.

"And food," added Jesse.

"I bet they have everything we need. We'll be okay," Sara assured Jesse as they squished and dripped with each eager step. "I hope Mom and Dad are okay somewhere else." She squeezed Jesse's arm. "And Scooter, too."

Sara signed them in at the check-in table. Jesse looked around the cafeteria. People filled the room. In the back, some people huddled near the few things they had left. Some curled up on cots with warm blankets. Jesse heard tired voices and children's whimpers.

In one corner people took sandwiches and drinks off a table. In another corner volunteers handed out dry clothing. Sara used the telephone while Jesse walked to the first-aid table. A volunteer cleaned and bandaged his bloody scratches.

When Sara rejoined him, she had a blanket around her shoulders and carried another one for him. "Here. Wrap up and get warm."

"Did you call home?" Jesse asked.

"Yes, but our phone is still dead."

Jesse looked distressed.

"But," Sara added quickly, "I got through to Dad at Gran's house. Mom was there, too. She couldn't get home because of the flooding."

"They're okay." Jesse breathed a deep sigh of relief.

"Dad will pick us up and take us back to Gran's," Sara continued. "He thinks he can find a way around some flooded streets, but it may take a while. Let's get some sandwiches. I'm starved!"

"Me, too," said Jesse. He felt hungry and tired, happy and relieved—and sick at heart. He missed Scooter.

The Day After

The Reyna family spent the night at Gran's house, which was on high ground. The next morning, the sun rose and began to draw the moisture out of the soggy ground. Schools and businesses were closed so that people could clean up.

The flooding had gone down enough for the Reyna family to inspect their house. They borrowed all of Gran's mops and pails and cleaning equipment and drove home.

Up and down their street, they saw neighbors lugging soggy furniture and rugs outside. Chairs, pillows, towels, bags, and baskets littered the yards. Muddy water had scrawled its brown signature on houses and cars.

"Phew! What's that stink?" Jesse asked. He sniffed his way to the flower bed in the front yard. There he found garbage and dead fish. "Yuck," he said. He turned to watch Mom unlock and open the front door.

"What a mess," Mom said quietly. She began filling a laundry basket with curtains, throw pillows, and anything else washable.

A coat of mud rose halfway up the first-story walls. The furniture, carpet, TV, and bookcases were covered with muck. Dad started piling up ruined books and hauling them to the curb.

Sara picked up her CD player. Muddy brown water ran out of it. "My new CD player!" she wailed. "I just bought it!"

"What about your CD collection?" said Jesse.

"Destroyed," said Sara with a gulp. "All my CDs were on the bottom shelf of the bookcase in the den."

"I'm sorry," Jesse told her. "You had a great collection."

"I'm sorry your belt buckle is gone," said Sara. "I know how special it was to you."

"It's okay," Jesse replied as they walked out to the yard. "It wasn't nearly as important as a lot of other things. At the shelter, I heard stories about missing children and missing parents." He kicked a can on the grass. "I can earn a new belt buckle next year, and you can buy new CDs. But you can't replace a family. I'm glad we're all still together." Jesse gave Sara a hug. Then he saw that the can had come to rest by Scooter's ball.

Jesse held his breath a moment to keep from crying. Then he tried to sound cheerful. "Maybe Scooter's just lost. I could put up signs. I could even put pictures of her on them."

Sara shook her head. "All the photo albums got soaked."

"All the pictures?" Jesse couldn't believe it.

"Dad said they were beyond saving. He put them in a trash bag out front."

Tears blurred Jesse's vision as he raced to the curb and dug through a garbage bag. He tried to shake the water out of a photo album. Big globs of mud splattered on the ground. He tried to pull apart photos, but they stuck and tore.

Jesse sank to the ground and closed his eyes. He could see Scooter chasing anything that moved. He could feel her messy kisses. He could hear her high-pitched bark. Tears fell like rain down his cheeks as he remembered Scooter floating away in the flood.

In his mind he heard her barking so clearly that he almost thought she was in the yard with him. He reminded himself it wasn't true. He opened his eyes and looked at the soggy photo album.

Suddenly a small cannonball raced toward him. "Scooter!" Jesse cried with joy as his dog flew into his arms. He hugged her tightly. She licked the tears from his cheeks. Then he heard Sara say "Hello."

A young boy answered "Hi." Startled, Jesse looked up. The boy was holding the hand of a tall man and carrying Jesse's belt.

The man said, "My son and I were looking for Jesse Reyna, but it looks like his dog found him first."

Jesse stood up. "How did you find me?"

The man put his hand on the boy's head. "Daniel here showed me your name on the buckle. I looked at the list of Reynas in the phone book."

"There are a lot of Reynas," said Jesse.

"Yes, there are," the man chuckled. "But today's newspaper showed a map of the flooded area. From the way your dog looked, I thought you two might have been separated in the high water. So we've been going to the Reyna addresses that were in the flood."

"Dad and I were playing catch, and your dog came out of the bushes to chase the ball," Daniel said. "She was all wet and muddy, so I washed her and brushed her." He held out the belt and buckle. "I saw your name on the buckle. You're an all-star. That's awesome. I want to be an all-star someday, too."

The man squeezed Daniel's shoulder. "My son is nuts about baseball. I don't know if other first-graders read the baseball scores each morning, but Daniel does."

Jesse slowly polished the buckle with his shirt, deep in thought. Then he handed the buckle to Daniel. "To me you're an all-star already. You brought Scooter to me safe and sound." Jesse shook Daniel's hand. "Thanks for bringing my dog back." Then Jesse turned and shook hands with Daniel's dad.

Scooter wagged her tail and gave Jesse a dog smile. "Now the whole family is back together," said Sara.

"Every one of us," added Jesse. He rubbed his face in Scooter's fur. "Family is the most important thing of all."